Building Character

Being Responsible

by Rebecca Pettiford

Bullfrog Books

Ideas for Parents and Teachers

Bullfrog Books let children practice reading informational text at the earliest reading levels. Repetition, familiar words, and photo labels support early readers.

Before Reading

- Discuss the cover photo. What does it tell them?

- Look at the picture glossary together. Read and discuss the words.

Read the Book

- "Walk" through the book and look at the photos. Let the child ask questions. Point out the photo labels.

- Read the book to the child, or have him or her read independently.

After Reading

- Prompt the child to think more. Ask: What kinds of things are you responsible for in your life?

Bullfrog Books are published by Jump!
5357 Penn Avenue South
Minneapolis, MN 55419
www.jumplibrary.com

Library of Congress Cataloging-in-Publication Data

Names: Pettiford, Rebecca, author.
Title: Being responsible / by Rebecca Pettiford.
Description: Minneapolis, MN: Jump!, Inc., [2018]
Series: Building character | Series: Bullfrog books
Includes index.
Identifiers: LCCN 2017025715 (print)
LCCN 2017036371 (ebook)
ISBN 9781624966446 (ebook)
ISBN 9781620318805 (hardcover: alk. paper)
ISBN 9781620318812 (pbk.)
Subjects: LCSH: Responsibility—Juvenile literature.
Classification: LCC BJ1451 (ebook)
LCC BJ1451.P48 2018 (print) | DDC 179/.9—dc23
LC record available at https://lccn.loc.gov/2017025715

Editor: Kirsten Chang
Book Designer: Michelle Sonnek
Photo Researcher: Michelle Sonnek

Photo Credits: Black-Photography/Shutterstock, cover (hand); Mirko Rosenau/Shutterstock, cover (flakes); S-F/Shutterstock, cover (fish); Ultrashock/Shutterstock, cover (bowl); Ermolaev Alexander/Shutterstock, 1; TinnaPong/Shutterstock, 3; wavebreakmedia/Shutterstock, 4; KK Tan/Shutterstock, 5; Photographee.eu/Shutterstock, 6, 23tl; Brian A Smith/Shutterstock, 7; Africa Studio/Shutterstock, 8, 12–13, 16–17 (background), 23tr; Pressmaster/Shutterstock, 8–9; Radius Images/Alamy, 10, 23bl; Dorottya Mathe/Shutterstock, 11; Nikola Solev/Shutterstock, 14–15, 23br; Gelpi/Shutterstock, 16–17 (foreground); Jupiterimages/Getty, 18–19; Sergey Novikov/Shutterstock, 20–21; ESB Professional/Shutterstock, 22 (top); FabrikaSimf/Shutterstock, 22 (bottom); Saturated/iStock, 24.

Printed in the United States of America at Corporate Graphics in North Mankato, Minnesota.

Table of Contents

We are responsible.

That means we can be trusted.

We do things we are supposed to do.

Bzz! The alarm clock goes off.

We make the bed.

6

We brush our teeth.

After school, we eat a snack.

Then we do homework.

We do our chores.

We set the table.

10

We feed the dog.

11

Do dirty clothes
go on the floor?

No. We put them
in the hamper.

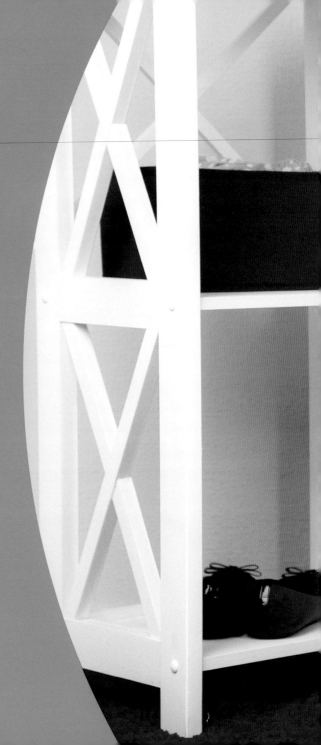

hamper

helmet

14

We wear bike helmets.
They keep us safe.

After we play,
we put toys away.

We keep our
room clean.

Chore Chart

Chores are small jobs you do to help out at home. Doing chores is a great way to show you are responsible. Make a chart to track your chores. Use the sample chart to help you.

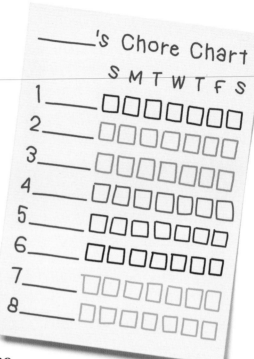

You will need:

- a sheet of paper
- markers
- small stickers (optional)

Directions:

1. At the top of the paper, write your name.
   Next to your name, write "Chore Chart" in big letters.
2. Under "Chore Chart," write the first letter of each day of the week.
3. On the left side of the paper, number and underline each chore.
4. Next to each chore and under each day's letter, draw a small box.
5. Each day when you have done a chore, put an "X" in the box for that day. You can also use a small sticker. You are responsible!

Picture Glossary

alarm clock
A clock that can be set to make a sound at a certain time.

hamper
A basket or other container that holds dirty clothes.

chores
Small jobs that you do often.

helmets
Hard hats that people wear to guard their heads from being hurt.

Index

To Learn More

Learning more is as easy as 1, 2, 3.

1) Go to www.factsurfer.com

2) Enter "beingresponsible" into the search box.

3) Click the "Surf" button to see a list of websites.

With factsurfer.com, finding more information is just a click away.

24